# Parable

# Parable

*Poems by Peter Karoff*

David Robert Brooks

Published by David Robert Brooks
P.O. Box 541106
Cincinnati, OH 45254-1106

ISBN: 9781625492302


Poetry Editor: Kevin Walzer
Business Editor: Lori Jareo

Visit us on the web at www.davidrobertbooks.com

To Martha and our lifetime of love

# Acknowledgments

The following poems have been previously published:

*Two-Part Harmony, Ways of Looking at a Wife*: To Woo & To Wed, Poseidon Press, 1992
*Stillness*: Just Money – A Critique of Contemporary American Philanthropy, TPI Editions 2004
*Conscience, Villanelle, Play On Words, Admonition, Time Stopped, Larger Than Life*: The World We Want – New Dimensions in Philanthropy and Social Change, AltaMira Press, 2007
*On My Youngest Turning Thirty*: The Brandeis Review
*Will, Play on Words*: Commonwealth Magazine
*A Higher Order of Thinking*: Martha's Vineyard Times
*Falco Peregrinus, A Perspective:* New England Aquarium Annual Report
*Easter Sunday*: Northeast
*The Writer's Notes On Incompatibility*: Private Clubs
*The Painting Within The Painting, Admonition, Listen To The Earth, So Long Ago*: St. Botolph Club Bulletin & 2011 Biennial
*The Geraldine R. Dodge Foundation Poetry Festival*: The Geraldine R. Dodge Foundation Annual Report
*Roof Tops, Yellow Light*: The South Florida Poetry Review
*The Train Ride Home*: Yankee Magazine


The author has been extremely fortunate to have as teachers Harold Bond, Dave Smith, Jane Cooper, and Daniel Halpern as well as Philip Levine who was fierce in his high aspirations for poetry in the life of the world. The author is also grateful to Perie Longo who was invaluable in the completion of this book.

Cover art: Dorothy Arnold

*A serious house on serious earth it is,*
*in whose blent air all our compulsions meet,*
*are recognized, and robed as destinies.*

"Church Going"
Philp Larkin

# Table of Contents

I

# Roses

I remember the rose that Patty
Gave me when my mother died.
A rose called Bonnie Lass or Sassy Lassy
Or Over the Rainbow, rainbow on an outgoing tide.
Let's make a new rose. Call it Sagamore Dawn,
Call it West Newton Hill, call it Caroling Party –
We wish you, we wish you a merry, merry….life
With hue and cry and joy, the floribunda of family
And all those roses that tell of being and loving a wife.
We do not design or choose our legacy.
It slips in, a bell-clear voice, and out, a certain shy glance,
Perfect bloom and private perfume of memory
Held as we would a beloved in a long, slow dance.

# Seasons of the Lily

The long, elegant arc of the day lily
over the back garden, bright stamens stab
the sun's heart, filaments retain heat
as petals embrace before their silent fall.

Thin lines of IV and oxygen sustain
the slight aspiration of her paper chest.
As fragile as stamen or pollen-bearing anther,
mother lies under the muted bluish lights.

"Sadie, Sadie, sweetheart, it's me George."
My father responds to each sound she makes.
It is only the echo of fluid in her chest
moving like an inevitable arrhythmic tide.

My mother loved the seasons of the lily
to minister over and mourn each fallen flower.
She is quiet now; the old watch the old
Until we all agree, there is no response.

# The Front Page of the Times

All night long rain has soaked the cushions
on the deck. A soggy Sunday morning in July.
Gardens, lawn, trees, The entire suburban world
lovely in gray except my king-sized dahlia.
It towers, blooms, a moon of yellow
beacon through sheets of rain,
as though rain could provide absolution,
benediction from an all caring, all forgiving God.

Is my glorious dahlia a last gasp genetic burst?
Is this fresh, washed world outside my window
a terrible illusion?  What seems pure and clean
is merely a wet, deep throated farewell kiss,
the last passionate spring of the last green July.

When Rilke wrote the word unsayable,
did he mean the way each wet leaf of the Copper Beech glistens?
Or is unsayable unthinkable, inconceivable,
the not possible, apocalyptic holocaust of everything green,
everything become unsayable?

If the sun comes out this afternoon,
a faint mist will rise,
moisture drawn back into the unsuspecting sky,
cushions will begin to dry,
dahlias sprayed again will keep beetles at bay.
I will be busy
Monday morning,
newspapers out to be recycled.

# October 18, 1988

The dahlias died last night.
The last huge blossoms burnt by frost
hang brown and grim,
like hoary praying mantis
towering over the back garden
where all summer long they presided
in brilliant, yellow majesty.

Dahlias dead, dahlias gone.
Today I'll put the garden to bed,
carefully fork each tubular bulb,
the sensitive bulbs
from the reluctant, nurturing earth,
earth still warm, rich, still worked by worms,
the not yet frozen, not yet wintered earth.

The bulbs must be dried,
the last green juice of summer drained
before they are set in paper bags
filled with white flecked vermiculite,
which even in the cool, dark cellar
sparkles with promises of spring.

# Lilacs on the Turnpike

*the lilacs performing like a circus*
*the lilacs speaking with my father's voice*
Felix Pollak

Between the Allston Toll booth
and Exit 17 comes the unmistakable
fragrance of lilac from scraggly
bushes between cracks in pavement
among warehouses and vacant lots
sweet grape royal purple medallion
floods my open car windows
washes my worldly weariness
a long day of shuttles Northeast
jammed un-air-conditioned planes
cabs in and out of megalopolis
it's late fog as thick as perfume
as a million million lush buds
from distant western suburbs
ride the heavy wet southwesterly
to converge in this unlikely spot
I breathe ever so deeply the air
the wet night life itself performing
speaking of sweet possibilities

# Year

*There and there again*
*A song faint in distant hills*
*A journey begins or ends*


The poems this year have been about dying,
Or rather about those who live in memory.
They seem to come in batches, a holiday sale
Of loss so you learn the language, bob and weave
Of prayer, awkward tiptoe of kindness
And you are left hollow, the hallowed ground
Shifts and prepares.

As time passes I keep meeting the past
On the corners of downtown streets.
Familiar faces, echoes of talk and work,
In my neighborhood, good houses, tall trees
Make a cathedral of wood and sanctuary,
In my dreams, more disturbed than ever,
In my ambition, unrelenting master still.

"I'm still proving myself after all these years."
"How long do we have to keep doing that?"
We both answer in one voice, "Forever!"
So we learn but little, live in the present tense,
Fill these small theatres of presumption
As though those who now live in poems
Have nothing to do with us.

# A Gentle Man

Many years ago
a gentle man
loved a woman
who loved her roses
more than she loved

A gentle man
who loved the sound
of an e-string
played with no regard

For regardlessness.
A hummingbird's
almost soundless
high-pitch whir of wings

The mildew black spot
of tears and apology
love does not die
comes to a quiet place
with a view of memory
in a sea of indifference.

After years of worry
a gentle man arrives
in the thickest thicket
where all the women
look alike and the violins
are made of rosewood.

# Benediction

Rabbi Al read
Joseph C. Corinha's name in synagogue
Even though Joe is not Jewish but Portuguese
Who smartly married a good looking Irish Catholic
Girl fifty-three years ago and counting.
Joe is a sick man and dying
Sooner than most of us who pray
On this Yom Kippurim day.
As Rabbi reads the long list of names
Of those who are ill, Jews and non-Jews,
Intermarried and remarried and those too young
Who may not live long enough to marry,
Everyone in Brandeis Hillel Levin Auditorium
Knew the prayer was not just for Joe.
And when Rabbi Al a tall imposing goodnik
Kind of man raises his arm high above his head
Like a prophet of old and slowly scans the room
Calling for others whose names should be said,
I am not alone in wanting to jump to my feet
To cry out every name I love, not alone
In wanting Rabbi Al to hold his benediction high,
Proclaim it loud, proclaim it to last the year.

# Bookends

Yehudi Menuhin Symphony Hall Boston April 1, 1948
Joshua Bell Granada Theatre Santa Barbara February 5, 2011

Exceptional day father closes the hardware store
We drive to Boston for great Jewish violin music
Maybe not as good as Heifetz father said
Yehudi Menuhin still a wonderment to behold
Hot Pastrami lean on rye G & G Delicatessen
Fortifies us Blue Hill Avenue to Symphony Hall
Famous American bastion for lovers of music
Come to hear Yehudi child-prodigy now forty-one
Music beyond my comprehension father transfixed
A glow glimpsed only on those rare occasions
Precious fiddle out of its case he plays so well
He never braved Brockton Civic Orchestra
Who surely would have made him first violin

I remember high notes on the edge of infinity
As they soar vast reaches of Symphony Hall
Statues Greek – Faun Bacchus Apollo stoic
On stage father shy Menuhin famously shy
Looks up with a soft smile signs our program
One day like this with my father but last night
Prodigal son Joshua Bell plays Schubert
An exuberant demon rubata rhythm beat
Perfect notes pierce us under chandeliers
Granada Theatre bronze sconces shimmer
My loved father sold stove linings grates paint
Wallpaper was in his heart of hearts an artist
Birthed in me yearning to be the same

# A Hierarchy of Blessings

The blessing of being a seeker
Metamotivation strives within

The blessing of individuation
Oh conscious unconscious be whole

The blessing of knowing each other
When I and thou become complete

The blessing of selective memory
You forget what you have forgotten

The blessing of God's presence
She is defrocked and disruptive

The blessing of silent sacred places
All you hear is the vibration of soul

The blessing of community
The sacred shining city on a hill

The blessing of doing the work
Dive deep your whole self in

The blessing of hope the great gift
Of being able to give

Final blessing is the first blessing
Our love our love of our family
Of the bitter-sweet world

# Sunrise Sunset — Rosarian at Work

*My mother Sadie's no. 498 record Book*
*80 sheets 7.5 in. 2 x 5 in.*
*F, W. Woolworth CO. New York, NY*

Worcester Flower Show, June 19<sup>th</sup>,
Mrs. O'Leary, Wien Street, West Roxbury
cordially invites dear Sadie our Mrs. K,
please come join our high society.

Come Sadie be dazzled by *Razzle Dazzle*,
by *Double Delight, by Rise and Shine* you
*Little Girl, you Bonnie Lass* you *Sassy
Lassy* who just loves *Betsy McCall*, loves

*Christine Vincent*, a real *Zinger*,
a *Hela Girl* who flies *Over the Rainbow*
while *Bing Crosby* croons my darling
*Darling Flame*, whitest *White Angel*.

Hybrid Tea, Floribunda, Grandiflora,
Polyanther trellised to the sky,
shrubs in brilliant flame roseates,
Heritage roses that bloom only once

Sadie, and don't forget minatures,
roses so sweet, so perfectly fun.
In the great American Rose Society
one looks for quality of color,

infinite hue, sculptured petals,
a scented universe that loves sun,
lives or dies by four to five hours
Sadie, morning sun by far the best

Dig hole 24" deep,
24" wide. Prepare the mix,
it's all in the recipe, Canadian
Moss (never Michigan peat),

Compost (apples), bone meal,
phosphate (one cup each),
Gypsum and Perlite or Terralite
or white-flecked Vermiculite.

Fill earth high around node,
over stems, Water slowly,
Epsom Salts (3 tlbs), Sulphur,
Chirlate, Limestone for each plant.

Hurry Sadie, showtime June 19th!
Variety of many petals take longer
to bloom the lower you cut. For show
cut weakest cane, deadwood.

Rosarian, hold your breath –
Pray it doesn't rain hard last week.
Wrap roses carefully, keep in water
for a smooth ride to Worcester.

And the winners are, a *Proud Land*
(two firsts), we live for *Mr. Lincoln*,
red bright red *Mr. Lincoln* (two firsts),

*Ivory Fashion*, a perfect *Pascal*.

Prize Winners all, you *Sonia*, you *Red Devil*,
you *Lemon Spice*, you *Yankee Doodle* dandy
and you pure *Shasta* you purest of white!
*Sunrise Sunset*, begin early, end late.

# Kindred Spirits

Hello out there
    All you kindred spirits
        Bring your sharp edges to the light
            Let's make a prism so bright
          You and I

A bottle of beer in one hand
    The sword of justice in the other
        We will make merry
            And bring the bastards down

The poetry of the moment
    Lives in the life of the man
        The poetry of the man
            Vibrates minds and hearts

In splendid castles in the air
    Sing out brothers and sisters
        Sing Emma Rosa Martin César
            Lazarus Parks King Chávez

Make a great crescendo
    Far beyond the rhetoric
        Abandon comfort
            Wake the soul that sleeps

Turn the turning loose
    The song is hope
        Balm to our troubled earth
            And lots of hard work
               For you and I

# Larger Than Life

When a good man dies
The earth nods, heaves a sigh
And goes right back to work.

Perhaps selling improvisations
Or taking on impossible odds,
Grandiose dreams by sheer force
Of will become reality.

Who ever would believe this script
In a world where the brisk business
Of birth, death, renewal and chance
Comes in on the money every time.

When a good man dies
The earth nods, heaves a sigh
And just goes back to work.

You can't trick fate
But you can mold it with passion,
Bend it by ambition
And turn it toward a better world.

# One Who Did Not Go Gentle

*for Lenny Zakim*

This one did not go gentle,
He went out with a roar
And he lived; well he lived like a Columbus
Whose faith shook the world.

This one lived in a fortress of love,
A thousand voices added to his own,
The strong beat of syncopated sound,
The surround sound of justice and joy.

This one went to the very edge
And faced the dybbuk of intolerance down,
Drew a line of right in the sand
And in the end stood his ground.

This one made us a great amphitheater,
A magnetic for generosity, for hope.
I feel his pull here, deep in the Negev,
Sun rising in a clear, cold, dawn.

Beer Sheva
December 3, 1999

# Tableau at Death Bed

All power comes down to one last gasp for breath

Stasis in the room holy silence a dreamy smile
Welling up of grief of story of beloved father
All the words spoken unspoken

Mom is waiting for him on the other side
She can see him coming
Takes his hand still firm grasp
Tough controlling loving grasp
On where to go what he wanted to be
What he wanted us to be

I learned never to do anything until
He told me to do it three times

I gave him a hundred ideas he took one
And then changed his mind
You did better than the rest of us

He knew the greatest gift
Passion to be the best that you can be

He loved Mom loved his family
Loved his work and he loved his God
With great force of heart and will

Legacy is to build it then give it back
is faith in a better way
is the generations forward
We are the soul of that legacy

# Villanelle

*for Henry Hampton*

The story is finished but it is not complete
We have listened, we have seen, we have been told,
Accolades, applause, are no mean feat

Nor celebration, nor awards. So why do we weep?
Weep for the archives, the untold metaphors of gold.
The series is finished but it is not complete.

In a great land, a country we so yearn to greet,
The comings, the goings of color, bright, black, unfold,
Accolades, applause, are no mean feat.

In life, in love, in passion, there is no retreat,
We go deep within our soul and pray it will hold.
The story is finished but it is not complete.

Was it today or yesterday the prize was sweet,
Pain and vision magnified a thousandfold,
Accolades, applause are temporal receipts.

Gentle spirit, castles in the air, these are concrete
Around us, surround us, told, untold and retold.
The story is finished but it is not complete.
Accolades, applause, are no mean feat.

# Sophie's Shadow

Look Bopa, my shadow!
Bright morning sun stamps
A perfect silhouette
Sophie's perfect curls
And my shadow too
Glide smooth on the dock.
Boats dance moorings,
Gulls bank in crystal air,
Shadows within shadows
Prance and make us tall.
We hold hands.

A century of life
Softly ends and I
Am much diminished,
One gentle pair of hands,
One more shadow gone.
Generations reconfigure
Out of air, out of loins,
Out of memory, out
Of each new morning
Shadows renew, one set
Of curls to the next.

# Saints & Sinners

Lots of sinners
But where are Angels of Mercy
When you need them –

Many do honest work
Leave the house before dawn
To sell money or even tall buildings

But a Saint
Does more than just show up
When a Saint walks in a room
Or on a city street
What you get is love

Not the syrupy kind
But gritty granular love
You can touch and touches you

Love is how those without face faith and home
Find all of those things

That's a Saint
Few and far between
Yet they exist
Their life and love the rarest gift

# Stillness

Kykuit
Pocantico


I sit at a writing desk on a raised dais,
A woman's portrait in a silver frame –
Gowned in brocade, a brilliant evening
Begun and ended long ago.

Sequestered high, a great corner room,
Leaded glass windows, the river
Distant and still. Lights on the far shore
Soften in the rose colored mist of dawn.

The castle keep of a storied house.
Something here wants to suspend time,
To pronounce the word *tableau*, pastoral,
Rolling hills, headland, river like a sea.

Something wants to call the question.
Could that possibly be snow? No,
Only the last silent fall of leaves
Blanketing the garden paths below.

Something here wants to call my name
As though I am ordained to answer –
Meaning, still beauty, hallowed ground.
Go forth – take the river to its source.

I am now the only air in the room.
What force of will made this house
Dispersed now where, what remnant
Of huge ambition, what atonement.

If I take it all in, argue the devil
His due, spend the bearer bonds
Of legacy down to my last breath.
Would that do, and for whom.

It is too easy here, too safe.
Something wants the silence to end,
Come chaos, a cacophony of voices
Descend. I sit, a tightly coiled spring.

# The Poetry of Politics

In the middle of the convention,
California out of control and Claude
Pepper grandstanding as usual.

> *I've been thinking about my mother,*
> *how she loved Sweet William.*
> *Most years she could not find them.*

Tell him to deliver and he's in,
If he can't he's out and we're fucked,
got it completely fucked!

> *The tiniest daisy-like petal*
> *gorgeous blue, pink, red, white*
> *with little tropical stalks. Lovely!*

If we lose prime time for his speech
that's two points in the Fall and that,
asshole, is the election.

> *Mother would stand in the garden*
> *on Highland Street, trowel in hand,*
> *like she was talking to the flowers.*

Look, he had his night, we met his kids,
He got his plane, ten million bucks,
What the hell else does he want?

> *This is the first year I planted*
> *Sweet William. I think they can*
> *be pinched like snaps to bloom again.*

I've put my candidate to bed.
It's 4AM, my body is still trembling
As though it didn't know we had won

As though it was afraid of power,
The cold glare of convention hall lights,
November's inevitable killer-frost.

# Connecting

A veritable network a work-net pre-internet
Rolla Doxy I'm only as good as in between
The dots I so love to connect I and thou
And you and yours add up and up
Perhaps that is all there is nothing personal
Offered or received did I choose this way
Or simply rise to the bait the demonstration
The expansiveness the self-importance
Of borrowed substance since I had none
How do you measure the chosen self
The satisfied glow of a big deal made
The occasional piece of critical legislation
A policy change for the good of mankind
A new neighbor well met a first job no less
All these wonderments all the time invested
Standing in stolen limelight such power
From me the supreme connector

II

# Easter Sunday

Kirby Studio
The MacDowell Colony

A small patch of blue, an otherwise gray day,
This is hard. I've never hidden so far away.
Towering white pine broods with memory.
Smoke from my fireplace swirls through trees
And quickly disperses any sign of work here.
As the last log becomes ember, signatures appear,
Hovering over bell clear notes and leaping words
That crowd this air like a thousand hummingbirds.
And what memory do you claim to miss?
Was it the mountain suddenly obscured by mist,
The sunrise service we never got up to see,
Or when we were all young and everything was we?

# Poem

Perhaps it was the cool air
We inhaled in huge goblets

Perhaps it was the tall trees
Pine needles cushion the forest floor

Perhaps it was the patch of blue sky
Sunlight filtered down on us

Perhaps it was your quick laugh
That took my breath away

Perhaps it was the contraband
The lie of the perfect day

# Ways of Looking at A Wife

The motion is always swift, always unexpected.
The great gangling, gawking heron suspended in blue
close enough to touch. Huge wings blanket the evening
and by virtue of tufted crest, yellow beak, blue throat,
we were immutably, precariously, nested.

How awkward a pair of amateurs we were,
fumbling in the grass, spilling wine and seed
while the stick-figure heron stood balanced on one leg,
listening for the inscrutable movement of tiny grubs,
the passionate positioning of the earth.

I hear the child's cry, your cry while bursting with milk.
The passage is always swift, always unexpected and far
from the sweet, sticky, lactose world that tastes
of chalk, the heron hesitates, spreads its massive wings
and I am jealous of this ultimate succor.

In the cold late of lonely night, a bottle of scotch
and the game is solitaire played hard. The card's sharp slap
on the kitchen table like the beat of angry wings on an earth
continually shifting in ways that are unexpected, until night
finally recedes in the pale hope of dawn.

The endless series of green walls, slanted ceilings,
attic windows that did not vent the cigarette stained air.
The bumbling, untrained hunter stumbles out the front door
and days become tiny dots on the horizon,
propelled by swift motion.


Of how the layers of chiffon unexpectedly swirled:
hair in high bouffant, a black dress, spaghetti straps,
lowest of décolletage, white shoulders, wide brown eyes
under bright chandeliers and our dreams of wild abandon
always unexpected.

# The Puzzle

The endless complexity of the puzzle
soothing in our dark, damp cabin.
Chagall's clown hides in jigsaw disarray.
A squall spills rain Southwest across the bay,
accelerates the tide, a red nun bows low
to a fisherman in a skiff, his yellow jacket
the only splash of color from our window.
I bow low to you, to the woman grown alone.
You stare at the puzzle. It stares back at you.
The blue clown, piece by piece comes alive
until there is one last figure, a ballerina.
You lift her carefully toward the light,
she slowly begins to turn, to pirouette
in the palm of your hand, twirling, spinning
rough edges smooth, the tufu flaring like
a tiny umbrella, like the beginning of a smile.

# Two-Part Harmony

A little piccolo and wheezy oboe
signal the start of my new day.
It's Martha snoring in early morning.

Like singing in the gently rolling sea,
Singing in the morning to Martha
Is like singing the best two-part harmony.

It's Martha making water.
She gropes back to bed, eyes shut tight
to extend that sleep-sense she so adores,
but I have long ago rearranged her life,
her pillow tucked-in tight like a body.

"Oh, Chrismas sakes, honestly, shush, shush, shs...."

She loves my break-of-dawn jocularity.
Singing in the morning to Martha,
Lying sturdy next to me.

Hello, what's that new song
taped to the refrigerator door?

"Morning cheerfulness, the principal cause
of husband beating."

You can tell that we agree,
Singing in the morning,
Singing la-de-da, Martha and me.

# The Writers Notes on Incompatibility

The drum-de-drum-dum-dum,
I hear your footsteps drumming
in hall, kitchen, dining room.
Your cup rattles the saucer,
a spoon stirs. I listen to
granulated sugar melt.
The screen door slides, a chair scrapes
on the deck. Phone rings and rings
four times before you answer.
Then you go to the bathroom,
flush-de-whoosh-de-swish-de-rush.
Most of all I hear you breathe,
all day long you are breathing,
huh-huh-whoo-whoo-ah-ah-hah.
Heart pumps, lungs expand, breasts heave,
Move ponderously up, down.
Crescendo fortissimo!
My concentration is shot.
I can't take it, I'm leave-leaving
for a ride with the top down,
iced-ice-cream-cone, drip, drip, drip.

# String Theory of Marriage

To infinity
A spider web rises from the forest floor

A tapestry
Tight wound colors warm a monastery wall

Capillary and Vein
Tight wrap of muscle and beat of vital organs

A woman hovers
Priestess with long hair in a Chagall print

Birth
Grow learn compressed to a single still shot

Tension
Of a cat's cradle turned into a trampoline

Supersymmetric
Partners bound by modes of excitation

Open loops close
Lovers accelerate and make whole numbers

Guitar and Lyre
The harmonics of a string being plucked

# Presence

I am writing because my memory has come back
Or playing tricks not that I was aware of its absence
Perhaps unaware is the point as in the book Presence
All about being in touch with oneself as the first step
To be truly present hard enough for dreamers
Impossible for self-absorbed ambitious drivers
Agents of change lab fanatics empire builders
All those who believe to do anything well requires
The relentless and since I am one so obsessed
It is disarming to say the least in midst of meetings
Critical matters of community and state suddenly
I am back in a cold Kerhonkson hotel room
Memorial Day weekend upstate 1956
There to work the crowd it was our first time
On a narrow bed the intensity electric
Indescribably intimate as fear dissolved
Safe haven found come home to all those dreams
I shudder now as then never more present

# Key West

*And yet, suppose some evening, I forgot*
*The fare and transfer, yet got by that way*
*Without recall, lost yet poised in traffic.*

"For the Marriage of Faustus and Helen"
Hart Crane

Suppose I forgot where the land ends
Or begins, suppose I lost my bearings
And my street address, my children's
Names, my access code, cell phone
Coordinates, what if the entire frame-
Work of an entire life disappeared
In the deep blue sea, man overboard
Somewhere near the Dry Tortugas?
What if I woke up in my own bed
And there I was, her breathing still
My constant company, suppose I
Forgot it all.

# The Naming of Names

Seth  Ethan  Joshua  Caleb
        It begins with the names
Deborah  Lorinda  Rebecca  Thomas
        This is how we begin to be
David  Paul  John
        The differentiation of names
Mark  Bruce  Tom  Julia
        The definition of a name
Gene  Larry  Lara  Karen  Sandra
        Each life unique to its own
Candace  Champe  Sarah  Mia
        How they join with others
Anna  Brad  Jeff  Leigh  Julie
        To begin again
Bobbie  Linda  Fran  Jill
        To name new generations
Alex  Claire  Maggie  Margo  Jacob
        Until they are here
        And we love them all

Begin with the naming of names
Without names there is nothing
Some barely have a name
Children of children
Fathers who do not know the name

So each day say one name

This day I say my granddaughter Lauren Paige

Now you say your name
        Know the name
        Love the name

# Living With Women

Such carrying on,
        the weeping and wailing
echoing across the lake.

Last moment of the last day
        of  Hillsboro Camp
for our twelve year old twins.

Campers and counselors
        huddled like Rugby players
unwilling to end the game.

A World Series of anguish,
        a Victoria Falls of emotion,
bonding beyond breath itself!

Was something wrong, I said,
        that only turned up the volume
a hailstorm of farewells.

And then the girls cried
        for two and a half hours,
All the way home!

I kept turning to my wife
        Something is terribly wrong!
She just smiled her Cheshire County smile.

# Yellow Light

I park by a white church
to wait for my son.
A small lamp in the church foyer
casts soft light on a pine floor.
This is an old part of town
that doesn't seem to change,
a village of gabled houses
clustered on a hill, tiny shops
hug the narrow road.
I stay a long time
stare through white lace curtains
as snow drifts across my headlights.

Early the next morning, my son and I
drive into the empty city,
tires whir on wet pavement,
windshield blurred by salt.
The sharp chill of wet snow
in our faces as we say goodbye
and slosh silently to work.
I think of warm yellow light,
the little church, the wood floor
worn smooth from steps
of so many fathers and sons.

# Walking in Madison Wisconsin

Walking in Madison Wisconsin
holding Jacob and Sophie tight
as though they were life itself,
I am struck by the disposition
of old West Side neighborhoods,
thousands of permutations
of so many families, so many lives,
and now my children's children's
voices join the chorus.

We perch, Jacob, Sophie and me
high atop Airplane House
fixed by Frank Lloyd Wright
in amazing perpetual flight
struck by how much
enhanced is our view of past,
present and future galaxies
just by walking with children
who make memory
as they bicycle around the block.

# On My Youngest Turning Thirty

*What I am is the way home*

*Air and Fire*
Wendell Barry

Fall, the Maple's leaves cascade down,
The Beech holds to the bitter end.
I turn the ground to plant Spring bulbs.
What presumption to that assumption!
More true is I haven't a clue
The longer it goes. What I miss most
Is the boy I knew yesterday,
Or yesterdays ago when we all
Lived in this white house, black trim...
Huge piles of pale yellow/red leaves,
Screams and laughter of my children,
A small black dog crazy with joy,
The endless work/work of it all,
The immense day-end satisfaction.
Like all memory, shaped, sustained,
It's how we take care of ourselves.
May it take care of you as well my son.

# So Long Ago

*A man and a woman*
*Are one*
*A man and a woman and a blackbird*
*Are one*

"Thirteen Ways of looking at a Blackbird"
Wallace Stevens

So long ago I've lost track of sequence,
So long ago a child's footprints in sand converge
As in a dream, so long ago blues, highs, lows, songs
Sung in kitchen-yellow chase the blues away.
Window-walls of bright light catch the Cardinal
Flash across the yard, our forty-year flash in a dash
Of salt, vinegar, sugar, and Classico Chianti
To the Cardinal, redder than dahlias burst in bloom,
Redder than the flush on my face, redder than blood
In my veins, the life force of our progeny
Bring tears, joy and grace to our own.

So long ago a crib in a dark stairwell, a baby sleeps,
A basement with no plan, no washing machine,
Living on bottle returns, on fumes of youth, of hope,
On Flying Horses, on shiny brass rings out of sight.

Once there was a blue park by a river, swings, tunnels,
Jack climbs the Beanstock, shrieks of hide and go seek.
Now lilies, heavy white blooms hung like chandeliers
Strain against tall poles, musk permeates the air.
A small white butterfly flits high into a tall tree
In the arboretum next door, and we are held hostage

In this place, its tapestry of story, event, remembrance,
Common, familiar, woven into things to us exotic.
In this house all the bad habits, all the old fears, lie just
Below the surface, all the unmet dreams absurd
In the irreversible flow of time of body and soul.

A man told me this week– "we are all beggars"– and it is so,
For salvation, for love, for so long ago.

# Words Not Spoken

*It would take forever to recite*
*All that's not new in where we find ourselves*

"In The Home Stretch"
Robert Frost

She a minimalist, he a maximalist.
Out of that comes a lifeline, a lifetime.

> *Most of all he shouts it shouldn't be dull!*
> *If you talked less, she says, perhaps...*

Amazing how opposites satisfy,
how irrelevant is nothing in common
after forty years of good morning
and good night.

A glass half-full, a glass half-empty,
mysterious beams energize membranes,
corresponding with each other and know
without knowing words that say it all.

Like Durrell's quarto vision of Justine,
same story virtually unrecognizable
as is ours.

> *Forget it, she's just a kid.*
> *No way she's grounded!*
> *Did I buy enough?*
> *Enough for an army.*

A kind of high ground, a reader's choice
for words you say and words you don't.

> *Is there cranberry juice in the refrigerator?*
> *Is our son well, or not?*

A certain slant of truth
catches you unaware
or music comes when least expected.

Heavy rain drums the Shed's roof,
thunder adds timpani where none is scored,
Brahms cradled in rain song,
the cadenza, a long high C.

Our cradle is memory
some of which we dare not rock.

> *It was this month a daughter died,*
> *I think of her every day.*

We know the lines by heart, stories not stated
not denied or lied comfort one another.

A chance glance across the hall,
yellow kitchen light on her face,
her grace you know better than your own
looks up at you.

Have you made the garden bigger, again?

> *Who can reason why Catmint runs wild*
> *or too many Oriental Lilies, says who?*

Long-term runs deep,
old movies seen over and over again,
grainy black and white still life
in sharp cinematic relief

beyond language,
our covenant of discovery,
of recovery, a son, a daughter, each other,
listening to words spoken and not spoken.

# The Train Ride Home

On Friday I go home by train,
moving in a kaleidoscope:
backyards, porches, rusted remains,
bicycles, oil drums, a father's hope

of a garden now overrun by weeds.
Windows on a thousand lives
before life's speed accelerated
and jets sliced the air like knives.

As the train rumbles in slow motion,
I see where New England began.
Suddenly there is the ocean
and winter ice extends the land.

The tiny terns are standing tall,
pencil legs casting shadows on ice.
Old wood boats in frozen overhaul.
I feel closer, a world made precise

by black-billed, arctic-bright swans,
a lone blue heron that wants my hand.
Then houses nested in pale sunlight
in Westerly, Kingston, Cranston.

A light goes on, a woman's face,
then gone. I think she has long hair.
Someone's billowing sheets erase
her silhouette hanging in the air.

III

# The Heron

This is where it starts
thin membrane of marsh
forest of tall grasses
tidal rivers and canals
and the heron slowly lifts
legs dangling a long neck
awkward like a camel's hump
upside down and the slow swing
of huge blue wings

The heron is the reward
I counted two today
standing like guardians
among cow egrets who punctuate
the text of the estuary,
slim commas made of chalk
while swans porcelain white
float on black winter water.

My train rumbles
across trestles of a bridge
disturbs the contemplation
the sweet organic wash of tide
Great Herodias takes to the air
languid and frosted like the grass
I imagine the call,
a low pitched croak
where it starts where it ends.

# Ospreys at Play

You know they were recruited
and given this perfect perch
with a straight shot
at the rise and fall of tide,
the abundant fish-hawk fishery
where Caleb's Pond hooks around
to the inner and outer harbor
on its way to Nantucket Sound.

They eye me with some disdain,
Stopped on the road below,
I hold my ground, stare right back
at these majesties
standing tall as if they owned
the place, and it was their road,
their pond, the whole topography
of ice-age land and sea made
just for them.

One by one they peel away
in long, low, confidant swoops,
their shrill, early morning warning
wakes the unsuspecting clams.
My clams!

peep-peep
beep-peep
peep-peep.......

# Admonition

Tell me stories of kinship
Of tropes of caritas effortless
Across a world stage
Tell me what you want to hear

In the face of fury
Moderation is a great fiction
A rhetorical stance subject to guile
Too much is at stake

What good are voices of good will
Sleepwalkers haunt my dreams
The cascade of moments has begun
This macrocosm this heart will break

Sometimes you are the only actor
Alone in the audience of your soul
Or your God if you admit to one
You cannot you dare not abdicate

# Listen to the Earth

September 2011

There is a prayer or sermon or speech.
In other words we fall back on words.
No matter how elegant or impassioned
They are weak. I am numb and dumb,
Staring into the face of evil.
All of us who sell widgets for a living
Or smoke and mirrors or even goodness
Have been stopped in our smart, fast tracks.
The elaborate machinery of life grounded,
The silly quarrels we have with each other,
The infatuation with our own importance
Absurd and pointless.

So listen to what the earth is saying,
Its multitudes, cacophony, infinities.
Alone we are nothing.  Oneness comes
When we close ranks, we link arms
And a community of the human spirit,
A fusion of brothers, sisters, colors,
Rises from the smoke and rubble
On the shoulders of the bereaved.
Become invincible, a mighty phalanx.

# First Responder

Whoever runs by first
And takes his shirt off

To know how much you
Love a place move far away

Bind wounds  stem the flow
Of blood and those tears

I see on the glistening cello
Bach's Partita in D soulful

Children's Chorus in memory
In prayer in thanksgiving

Entire world a narrow bridge
Good Samaritans on patrol

God heals the brokenhearted
Kill a soul kill all of mankind

Run with endurance the race
That is set before us

City a perfect state of grace
In a culture of civic faith

Crowds become community
The instinct is kindness

Everyone has been touched
With the hope of tomorrow

His sign said "No more
hurting people – Peace"

Whoever runs by first
And takes his shirt off

They who will run again
You who will run again

# A Higher Order of Thinking

Convergence somewhere
Between idea and dream
As insight once formed
Sends us soaring free.

I remember the movie
About Vincent Van Gogh,
How the cry of creativity
Made us cry.

We still do,
Drawn by a powerful
Magnetic field of dreams
Full of remembrance.

We stumble over foils
Of our own make
Despite proclamations
Of making it new.

I need a kick-start,
A word, perhaps colors
Off the deck, field, pond,
The meadow beyond.

Three shades of green,
Still water vaultiest blue,
Or whispers of cloud
From the ferry to town.

This week we grieved
Who was left to grieve.
Locked gates of memory
Opened flood tide wide.

# There Was Wind

There was wind,
that much you could see
the night fire rained from the sky,

rained like bright shiners
unmaking the gospel. Aye
it was the work of the devil

whose hot aluminum breath
blew over the countryside
scorched land and hearth.

There was time
that much we thought we knew
as oil spilled plenty of time

to lay a million mile boom,
a thin necklace, white
against the throat of earth.

Aye it is the rummy devil
mimicking flightless birds,
oil spread on the shore of time.

# Once a Moon

This is no false moon
A Winter Solstice
At lunar perigee
Arrives but once a century
Moon over millennium
Close as one can get

In 1866
The Lakota Sioux
Under just such a moon
Wyoming prairie lit like day
Staged retaliation
From the depth of desperation
As close as they ever got

Tonight's 5pm Delta shuttle
And the heavy orange moon
Lift into a crystal-clear night
An odd couple traveling
A coastline I love just
As apogee reaches closure

East of Boston we circle
Wide and bank low
Over a shining silver sea
There – right of the wing
Immense cold white Nova
Of hope as close as one gets

# Time Stopped

Time stopped at 4am. I continue to breathe.
Sheer white curtains move in a slight breeze,
Nothing else the same when time stood
Suspended, disturbingly, unnervingly, still.

It happened once before sailing east all night.
We had made good time just past Matinicus,
Rock guardian to the great Bay of Maine,
Muscongus, Penobscot, and Scoodic beyond.

I was at the tiller as the glorious sun
Rose huge, shining gold, then incredibly stops,
Vibrates the horizon, unsure whether to lift
Into the clear morning sky or roll along

The lip of the earth into the void of another
Universe or just slip back down, leave the world
Bereft, lit by pale moonlight or forever dark.
Terrifying, but the sun slowly began to climb,

And the clock moved finally after what seemed
Eternity past 4am, but what if time did stop
For white cells, red cells, children who stay young
Forever we hold on to them, as to life itself.

# Office Hours in Hartford

*At twelve, the disintegration of afternoon began.*
*The sky was blue beyond the vaultiest phrase.*
                                    Wallace Stevens

A great northerly flow of air
Drives heavy rain from Boston –
It is early morning, cumulo-nimbus on a roll.
I come to visit actuaries
Glass and steel-encased gnomes
Who calculate future shock-waves
Of the greater tundra-driven winds,
And full moons that fuel flood tides
As though data alone could predict
The survival of life on earth.
I think of him on just such a day
Walking in topcoat and bowler hat,
A gray-suited guardian of the money pile
Who parades alone the leaf-blown streets,
Amidst memos and stifled air
Of the all-afternoon conference
Delineating wind-whipped odds.
Was his eye to a window drawn
To mountainous tumult of cloud
Racing across a cerulean sky?
Was this his practice that reduced
All phrases to purest harmonium?

# The Moral Amateur

Sins of omission
And commission
Practiced daily.
A four-way mirror
Reflects a veritable army
Of the non-commissioned,
Lonely sentries who stand
On the outermost banks.

Technological diffusion
Main street to Wall street,
Asynchronistic confusion
Publicly offered
Lurches out of control.
A royal straight flush
Flushed down the drain,
The proverb, the proverbial

Astronauts, diplomats,
Forget-me-nots unite.
Big-bang, implode, reload,
Ecological engineering
Gone haywire sucks
At hydroelectrics, hearts
Of darkness buried under
Mountains of debt and debris.

What's left is banality,
Earth's inevitable meltdown,
Crown princes in their yachts
While Noah shrugs and laughs
At the last raft of dollar bills.
We practice sins of the father,
Call the body politic to order,
Rhetoric, clarion call, last call!

# Coast to Coast

Coast to coast
In a haze, a daze
Of days, crying jags
Of singular proportion
Hold depression at bay.
The cargo is precious
For the precious few who care.

I care, we all care,
The monumental I
And my partner cares
As we are caretakers –
The truly lonely have none.

Coast to coast,
East to west
In search of destiny
Like Paul of Tarsus
Who gave as good as he got.
My day starts early and I work
Until I can't think. Everything
Else is on hold. Everything!
This is how one builds a church.

Coast to Coast
Like millions before,
Conestoga wagons took months,
Fibre optic cables milliseconds.
It is 9:30pm San Francisco time.
Were I in Boston
I would be a year older.
Only a few hours grace
Remain, remaindered
To the clang of cable cars
Outside my window,
The rumble, grumble, scratch
Of a city, a history, a life.

# Bitter Without Sweet

Election 2012

The bitter without the sweet
A fight to the death a war
As in Saving Private Ryan
Take no prisoners
These politics are to die for

Suddenly in the tree above
The presence of a large bird
Entry exit simultaneous
Briefly glimpse the hawk
It swoops and is gone

Leaves still trembling
I tremble too
In the rubble of conscience
Bits and pieces of soul
Every neighbor a stranger

And sweet justice a fugitive
From the camp of whoever wins

# Conscience

*..caught in the dangerous traffic between self and universe.*
Stanley Kunitz

I carve out a small space, a nest
Of sorts and lie my conscience down.
As a gift it bears little resemblance to
The madness around me, those who think
They know everything, those who despair.

My own absurd, hesitant, presumption is hope.

I watch the Osprey hunt the harbor at dusk,
It soars and glides to a frantic wing-beat
And like an acrobat hangs in mid-air
As flashes of silver scales below
Signal time to make a precision dive.

My own hesitant presumption is hope.

As an infant flails, wails, loss of womb,
Its wet, loud, pronouncement – I am here!
My conscience, not newborn, nor single-
Minded like the Fish Hawk, hears the cry
Of the wounded heart.

My own presumption is hope,

Even as deadly fog shrouds the backstage
It is no match, these awakenings are legion,
New dimensions of spirit and soul
Rise from sweet hearth and beloved earth,
Feminine and Divine.

My own hope

Lies in Mahler's $1^{st}$, from minor to major,
From darkness to Frère Jacques. So rise
Tired traveler, renew, seek secret places,
The great percussion of possibilities within.

IV

# Notes From the Deck

bee after honey in my tea
on a day associated with Rosh Hashanah
a cerulean September day
warm after night frost dulled the dahlias
a half shade brown

the front lawn considers recovery
from last week's wedding
so do we

what did the rabbi say

no wonder I feel poor

bee discovers a mother lode
and hovers over my cup
like a cookware salesman on a cold call in Keene NH

the rabbi said Dad doesn't look ninety

what is the income steam from poetry

I charge $500 a word
$500 a word – you can't get much work at those prices
I don't need much work at those prices

wash honey and lemon
from the blue ceramic

# Play on Words

In a good play on words
Ideas seem to just emerge,
Fully formed long lyrical lines
From the chamber of a brilliant mind.

Hah! Don't believe it my friends!
Chaos– thousands, thousands of words,
Ideas, theories, notions carom off walls,
Tumble off the backs of one another.
Some drift lazily like hot-air balloons,
Bump gently up against the ceiling
Or as bats do hang upside down.
Others dash madly about like sperm
In passionate search of an egg to fertilize,
While those deemed worthless fall away
And die a slow lingering death.
How sad is the dismembered idea!

Once in a great while an event occurs.
Call it metamorphosis, transformation,
Inspiration out of the incomprehensible–
An idea is born and pops into plain view.
Such joy in the chamber of the mind that night
As all of those still stuck in chaos party
In everlasting hope their turn will come.
The birth of a good idea is rare indeed.
Even rarer are those who have the gift.
To one who does, we say Salut!

# Commit a Random Act of Kindness

Billboard  Massachusetts Turnpike

Friday 6:08 AM bill-bored
nonsense on auto-pilot
office stuff roars red-line
right through the weekend
so kill-it & I shall absolutely
randomly commit all sorts
of sordid desperate foolish
whimsical acts of mind-matter
fleshed haphazard soon forgotten poetically benevolent
known for her many unknown
kindnesses aimless unconnected
to truth flames winds change!

# Ultrasound

amazing
how my inner space
so resembles a wormhole in outer space

how un-intimate
the young doctor's intimate exploration

how fluid the fluids
swirl flickering on the TV monitor

how the dim blue light
around each changeling nook and cranny

amazing
quick the fall from grace
this silent movie with aliens dancing

# The Painting Within the Painting

*A sonnet is a moment's monument*
*A sonnet is a coin: its face reveals*
*The soul —*
　　　　　　Dante Gabriel Rossetti


A still life deceives the viewer it is not so still
Stage set ubiquitous dark green cloth ingredients
Three onions perhaps a good neighbor lent
One sits lonely in a large pot waiting to be filled
Center right a marvelous vessel or urn ornamental
Copper or bronze or brass whatever alloy opulent
Shimmering Sultan-esque a successful experiment
The eye is beguiled we are captivated we are thrilled

Yet peel back the onion's countless layers of skin
And our tears fall and weeping and wailing begins
Bronze is brown copper and one-third tin while brass
Yellow copper and zinc hardness and impudence
But within the cacophony is music let it commence
I say put the artist back to work — here is your brush!

# Rooftops

I can barely see the men
In their high rubber boots
working hot tar with rakes,
steam rising from the roof
into the blue cathedral sky.
Men floating in, out of mist
that billows and evaporates
around dark silhouettes.
Here on the eleventh floor
Of this pre-war building
it's the top of the world:
blackened by soot, buttressed
by the weight of old brick,
a kind of rooftop fortress.
It oddly seems of a piece
without blocks or streets.
A landscape of small doors,
sheds, wires, water-tanks,
pipes twisted like gargoyles.
Not Utrillo's Paris rooftops
or Mary Poppins' chimneys,
these roofs thrive on deals,
secrets, air-raid wardens
with thermoses of coffee
hunker down for the night
among smells of urine, cat.
Who are these men,
hammering, fixing, smoking
while leaning over a wall
looking for something below,
perhaps what brought them here

for distance, safe-haven,
a vaultiest high, azerous.
I wish I was with them.
We would work the sky together,
dangerously innocent
of death-defying leaps,
men who want to be alone,
alone with their dreams,
men work the working roof,
weathered as any wilderness.

# Surrealism in the City

Waiting for an unsafe elevator
in arguably the worst building
in New York City of many
lousy buildings two men jammed
in a dirty littered poorly-lit lobby
each trying to ignore the other
surly process-server sort of fellow
and me when a heavy-set woman
joined us and all of a sudden
her head reflected in a mirror-
wall of a hundred mirrors
the woman's image endlessly
repeated smaller and smaller
until a dusty dot disappears
on a far distant horizon
of course the other man and me
followed rippling off endless off
of surrealism in the city story
and so I said look at that will you
we've gone forth and multiplied
Hallelujah said the woman shit said
the man we all burst out laughing
having a grand old time until
the slowest elevator in New York
finally came and delivered us

# The Geraldine R. Dodge Foundation Poetry Festival

I left,
left in the middle of Mark Doty's reading
in a mad dash to catch the last plane out,
left a thousand poets hanging on each word,
left a beautifully lit stage, the absolute perfect
acoustics, left before Philip Levine even read
who would have yelled had he seen me slip
like a thief out the Main Tent into the night,
Where the hell are you going, are you so stupid!
So stupid trying not to get lost, this friendless,
endless labyrinth of roadway, and then flying,
I had this sudden sense of loss, of having left
behind a higher eloquence, a theater of voice,
the one place on planet earth true poetics,
the underrepresented passion was building,
powerful, magnetic, pulling all the poet spirits,
written, unwritten, million and millions
of particles descending in brilliant metaphor
of hope, of community, convening like nothing
ever in Northern New Jersey

# Falco Perigrinus, a Perspective

I'm thinking indemnification,
worrying the irrevocable loss.
True I do have a State Street/Custom House
point of view, bonds routinely issued,
richly resourced, asset guaranteed,
but let me tell you, the fish, schools of fish
that swam thick often swim no more
even the harbor's deep outermost part.
I miss their blue and silver shadows,
their soft, seamless, choreography.
Someone must stand surety here, but who?

This morning, to clear my head, I fly high.
I love the brilliant Northerly days,
sweeping, soaring, on strong winter winds,
higher, higher, air become so thin,
sheaves of particled gold enough to hold,
literally one can see forever —
Nahant's prim little nose, east to Cape Ann,
Casco Bay, south to P-town, Cape Pogue,
Nantucket's soft shoals, the tip of Long Island.
What a gift, this ice-age land meets sea
all sparkling so gloriously!

# Reconciliation

A tough old bird
One legged gray mottled feathers
Seagull owns a coral rock
Absolute dead low tide
I am clearly too close for comfort
Bird annoyed loud squawks
Slow awkward lift off

At LAX chaos scramble
Heft heavy bags on the Hilton bus
A woman pushes and says
"You're pretty strong for an old guy"
Her husband – I think – laughs –
"She can only lift 100 pounds"
"Time to trade her in" I say

First light at 4:30 far too early
All around awake by what call
What cricket or hoot owl
What aspiration gives it up today
What beach walk beats the tide
When do you trade in
An old bird or an old guy

# Will

Governments fail from lack
Fortunes rise and fall
And great art is made by force of

You won't find will in resumes
It isn't always noisy
And often lies deep

Obsession while not will
Is part of the intensity
Which is a precondition

Conception is nice
But doesn't express will
While execution  oh yes

The ah ha components are
Passion and huge ambition
All over a good idea

# If I Had More Time

If I had more time I would write a poem
But my quiet morning in the sun mountains
On one side ocean the other got swept away
A dizzy array of significant calls and emails
In fact the whole week and next
A kind of blur so the pressing poem *Presence*
*Stillness* my mother's favorite *Sassy Lassy* rose
Was not written and all of a sudden December
The voice of my teacher Mr. Levine rings out –
"What the hell are you doing with the writing –
Why did I waste my time on you why indeed you!"

If I had more time I would write a poem
The years flowed now ten years now twenty
There were of course occasional poems
No coronations like Auden but wedding birth
Death but not the unspoken poem passionate
About the hurt world of a hungry child
Or Abraham's poem of brothers and sisters
Or the deep poems of inner revelation
Or the poem of magic dolphins who shadow
A lone walker on a Pacific beach at low tide.

If I had more time I would surely write a poem
Until one day Levine called out of the blue to say –
"It isn't finished this poem called ordinary life
Poems are hard to finish so keep pushing
That is your job!" So it finally dawned on me
What I do what we all do is write the poem
Every day we write the observant poem of life
You see it isn't a matter of time but compassion
Call it community or hope or faith or call it love.
That is the flow that is the poem.

# Stopped

*Failing to fetch me at first keep encouraged*
*Missing me one place search another*
*I stop some where waiting for you*
'Song of Myself'
Walt Whitman

Stopped dead in my tracks
No tally is this no pussy-footing around truth
Say it like it is she passed the place where I stopped
Was I invisible or she spirit-less gave it up had it with all
the hyper-medicalization the surround sound beep beep
Intravenous malfunction gone hay wire like a victim
Of some random design despite presumptive care hovering
The whole elaborate expense useless impervious to self
Object of irrelevant data I search for her I wait
Some where herself  I know better than my own
At the end she was transfigured wide brown eyes
Stare into the ether beyond comfort beyond words
beyond all these many years all worth waiting

# Oh Cecelia Oh Elisabeth

They materialized magically from the congregation
Who knew they were there to lead us in communal song
Two sopranos two contraltos one tenor a chorus no less
Holding forth Joni Mitchell Both Sides Now as though
They had practiced for hours and a good thing it was
We could hardly sing a note so overwhelmed by loving
Martha in the morning Martha in the evening a cascade
From all sides a lifetime of sighs holding on to each other
How she loved a soprano's gifted voice singing carols
Christmas made magical meaning elevated to the highest
And we belong to it all gathered in this precious space

# Sinking In

*I am thinking like a poet – her absence must almost be a presence*
Barbara Lawrence

Absence is not the opposite of presence
You can be present but still be absent
How many times have you and I heard that
And one can be present even in absence
In a court of law it is called "in Absentia"
From the Latin convicted or acquitted
But nowhere in sight but you are in sight
What is absent is the idle conversation idling
Along just the two of us a steady hum
Of perfect-pitch music of the smallest
Of things the thing become the thing
Minutia of one's life integral to the other
Silence fills the empty house filled to the brim
With you with the brilliant colors you chose
The art the glass the bright reds and blues
All things curated with your loving soul
Present and absent takes me sinking in

# Parable

Here I sit, on a rock by a still pond. It is early evening, the last rays of the setting sun filters through the tops of the trees. Too early for the Loon, the Cardinal calls out for its mate as the woods settle in, ready to transition to night.

Across the pond in a small cove, I can just make out a Great Blue Heron balanced on one leg. I imagine the concentration, the analysis and observation of the pond's murky bottom.

I sink deep into this place, wet and primeval with almost infinite shades of gold and green, with moss and lichen that covers the ground and wraps around the base of trees. Water bugs scoot around the rock outcropping where I sit, moving rapidly in great number and variety and I imagine bass and pickerel lurking lazily below.

It all seems like a gift and the words from an old Shaker hymn float into my head:

> 'Tis the gift to be simple,
> 'Tis the gift to be free,

I have been given the gift of solitude tucked away in the deep woods, alone with mind and spirit and peace while the world in which I live and work in all of its tumult, energy, pain, and joy, seems far, far, away.

> 'Tis the gift to be simple,
> 'Tis the gift to be free.
> 'Tis the gift to come down
> Where we ought to be,

I sit on a rock by a still pond in the midst of a perfectly balanced natural system, one that is harsh and gentle, competitive and yielding, rigorous and forgiving, pragmatic and magical. A system so, so, violent and still capable of producing serenity. You would not have the one, the beauty, without the struggle of the other.

Nature is immensely complex, more complex than the most advanced technology and requires a multitude of collaborative and interdependent initiatives to survive and prosper. All of this happens intuitively without doubt or hesitation. What seems to underlie nature is an incredible amplitude and abundance as though the plan were over-engineered, and unless man interferes, a remarkable re-generative capacity to carry-on, and on, and on.

Nature is anything but neat with constant spillage and what seems like error and waste, but what wins out in the end is this magnificently generous system yielding one gift after another.

> And when we find ourselves
> In the place just right
> 'Twill be in the valley
> Of love and delight.

Something startles the Heron. It awkwardly gathers up those long, spindly legs, and hesitates for a moment as though reluctant to let go of the intrigue of the pond's muck and mud. The great bird lifts, huge wings cast a muted shadow on the water, and flying straight towards my rock gracefully swerves off to the right, disappearing among tall pines along the shore.

These are gifts given to me, a still pond, a Heron, Monadnock Mountain, tall marsh grass, dunes overlooking South Beach, the immense, undulating sea beyond– all, all, valleys of delights.

When true simplicity
Is gain'd
To bow and to bend
We shan't be asham'd

On my rock by the still pond the water mirrors nature but so much of my own world is reflected here as well. My world has all of these same characteristics, sadness, suffering, despair, chaos, in-equity and certainly violence. It also has the same capacity for re-generation, for hope, for beauty, for joy, and even peace and solace. But where the natural world knows what to do, and is driven, governed and balanced solely by instinct, my world is not intuitively balanced at all and constantly demands other more elusive elements, courage, patience, and especially will and love. Perhaps even more difficult, knowing what is right and good to do. Without will and love, without a sense of the just and the unjust, without confidence in ourselves, we are at risk, on the edge, ready to fall into a void or even worse spin completely out of control taking those we love with us.

To turn,
Turn will be our delight
Till by turning, turning,
We come round right.

My will is weak and tempered by what the philosopher calls *natural shame* from within, and *moral shame* from those who know me. I am often afraid, wracked with self-doubt, and not sure what is right and good. I want to love but that requires much courage, and a giving of myself fully while risking rejection. You see, both will and love are acts of selflessness, of generosity.

What do I seek, what do I yearn for?

I seek a rock by a still pond.

The evening is rapidly becoming night and all around is a softening of sound, wood and sky and I think of *Dusk* as I wrote this for my Grandson Jacob:

> There is evening and evening song
> sun goes down and takes the light along
>
> and at a certain moment difficult to define
> day or night light or dark is hard to find
>
> instead you see a milky misty shadowy fall
> softly sending goodnight kisses to us all

I sit on my rock by the still pond and dream of "goodnight kisses" sent to us all, of "valleys of love and delight", of finding oneness of mind, spirit and self, of finding the will and the courage to love, to do the right thing, and I am filled with a powerful yearning to be the best that I can be, to do the work it takes to turn, to "come round right".

As I sit on my rock by a still pond, how clear it becomes. We are all nurtured by this generous world and we must in turn make it so. We must make it so!

> 'Tis the gift to be simple,
> 'Tis the gift to be free.
> 'Tis the gift to come down
> Where we want to be,
> And when we find ourselves
> In the place just right,
> 'Twill be in the valley
> Of love and delight.
> When true simplicity is gain'd
> We shan't be asham'd,
> To turn, turn will be our delight
> 'Till by turning, turning we come right.

# Notes

*One Who Did Not Go Gentle* – Lenny Zakim was the Executive Director of the Anti-Defamation League in New England.

*Villanelle* – Henry Hampton was the producer of the award-winning PBS documentary *Eyes on the Prize – A History of the American Civil Rights Movement*.

*Stillness* – Kykuit is the great house at Pocantico, the Rockefeller Family estate on the Hudson River in Tarrytown, NY.

*Easter Sunday* – The MacDowell Colony in Peterborough, New Hampshire, is the oldest artist colony in the United States.

*Words Not Spoken* – the Durrell reference is to the four novels that comprise The Alexandrian Quartet – *Justine, Balthazar, Montolive,* and *Cleo* in which the same story with the same characters is told from multiple and wildly different perspectives – the "Shed" reference is based on Tangelwood, the summer home of the Boston Symphony Orchestra in Lenox, Massachusetts.

*Office Hours in Hartford* – Wallace Stevens' first book was entitled *Harmonium.*

*Parable* – The Shaker song *"Simple Gifts"* was written in 1848 by Joseph Brackett Jr., a member of a Shaker community at Gorham, Maine. The song was largely unknown outside Shaker communities until Aaron Copeland used its melody for the score of Martha Graham's ballet Appalachian Spring first performed in 1944. Copeland used "Simple Gifts" a second time in 1950 in his first set of Old American Songs for voice and piano – The terms *natural shame* and *moral shame* come from the work of Harvard philosopher John Rawls.

# About the Author

The poems of Peter Karoff (1937–2017) have been anthologized and published in various periodicals. *Parable* is his first book of poems. He wrote extensively on the moral and ethical dimensions of philanthropy and was author of *The World We Want – New Dimensions in Philanthropy and Social Change* (AltaMira Press, 2008) and *Just Money – A Critique of Contemporary American Philanthropy* (TPI Editions 2004), both of which included poems.

He was a graduate of Brandeis University (1959), and completed an MFA in Writing from Columbia University in 1988, where he received the Benjamin Burns Poetry Prize. In 1989 Peter was made a Fellow of the MacDowell Colony in Peterborough, New Hampshire. He received an Honorary Degree, Doctor of Humane Letters, from Lesley University in 2002 and in 2006 became a Purpose Prize Fellow.

Made in the USA
Lexington, KY
06 September 2017